Poems for Dylan

Vernon Watkins

First impression—2003

ISBN 1 84323 236 7

This book is published with the support of the
Arts Council of Wales.

Gomer Press would like to thank Jeff Towns Dylans Bookstore for
providing the Vernon Watkins typescript and 'The Times' obituary.
Similarly, Bernard Mitchell for his assistance with the front cover photograph.

CONTENTS

OBITUARY IN *THE TIMES*
BY VERNON WATKINS
Tuesday, 10th November 1953

Mr Dylan Thomas: Innovation and Tradition

Mr Dylan Thomas, the Welsh poet and story writer, died yesterday in New York at the age of 39.

Dylan Marlais Thomas was born in Swansea in 1914. He was educated at Swansea Grammar School, where his father, who died last year, was senior English master. He began writing early, and at the age of 12 he was able to show his parents and his friends poems which seemed to have no direct ancestry in English poetry. These poems already bore the marks of that strong individuality in pattern-making and choice of language which was to distinguish him from all his fellow-writers in maturity.

He had developed at school a passionate feeling for language which was sharpened and intensified by an acute destructive judgement. He took no reputation for granted. He approached the great masters of his art with an impudent suspicion, because from the first, he distrusted the academic approach. Yet, when they had walked with him through the furnace of his own imagination and emerged unscathed, there was no man who loved them more. Indeed, no poet of the English language has so hoodwinked and confuted his critics. None has ever worn more brilliantly the mask of anarchy to conceal the true face of tradition. There was nothing God ever made that Dylan Thomas, the revolutionary, wanted to alter. The careful compounder of explosive imagery believed only in calm.

At the age when Rimbaud wrote his poems Dylan Thomas had left school and was working as a reporter for the *South Wales Evening Post*. His first poems, apart from those which had appeared in the school magazine, which he edited, were printed in the *Sunday Referee*. He had also at this time begun to write short stories. Then, finding his newspaper work and his own writing incompatible, he left the newspaper and lived for a time in London, sharing a flat with two of his Swansea friends. Here his literary work continued, and developed rapidly his researches into the power of language. He directed his various gifts to the concentration of verbal energy in a pattern at once musical and compact. His poems reflected the fiery, Blake-like passion of his vision, while his early stories explored the relation between immediate reality and archetypal symbols.

The Early Poems

When in 1934 Dylan Thomas's first book, *Eighteen Poems*, was published, its impact was immediate and profound. It was at once realized by discerning readers, among whom Edith Sitwell was one of the first, that this poet had created an idiom; that he had disturbed the roots of our language in an organic way and given it a new vitality. There was nothing stale or imitative in the book: the poems were fastidiously worked; they were poems of a man who had listened, not once but a hundred times, to the minute effects of words. It is true that still, in 1936, when this was followed by *Twenty-One Poems*, the poet had not yet found his most permanent and compelling medium of expression. Yet there was nothing topical in his work. The most mistaken of his admirers were those who loved it for its novelty. It was, even in its final phases, an ancient poetry not rejecting antiquity for the present but seeking, with every device of language, the ancestry of the moment.

'The Map of Love'

If the poetry of his first two books had been admired for the wrong reasons, the poems printed in his third book, *The Map of Love*, could hardly suffer the same fate. Whereas the first book leaves an impression that the poet could extend his stanzas from the fund of invention and verbal felicities at his command, and that the same prescription could produce new poems, there is no such impression left by the poems in *The Map of Love*. Each is an experience perceived and controlled by the religious sense and each answers its own questions. He had pared his imagery without losing any of its force; and these poems close with the statement at the end of the poem for his twenty-fourth birthday:

> In the final direction of the elementary town
> I advance for as long as forever is.

The Map of Love contained also a set of stories which were clearly the work of the same hand, and these were followed two years later by the humorous stories, in quite a different vein, which Dylan Thomas collected under the title of *A Portrait of the Artist as a Young Dog*. These stories, about the poet's own boyhood, written from direct experience in Swansea and the Gower peninsula, may seem to some to carry the fault of exaggerated statement, but they are as true to life as his own personality was to his friends.

Innovations in the Stanza

It is, however, upon the poems in *Deaths and Entrances* (1946) and the few poems of the slim volume *In Country Sleep* published in America in 1951, that his reputation as one of the greatest masters of English poetry is likely to rest. In these, Dylan Thomas had not only used to perfection the idiom he himself created but has invented stanza forms which are themselves organic and which redouble the force of the entire poem. These poems form the final section of his *Collected Poems*, published last year.

During the war Dylan Thomas, who was always interested in the cinema, made several documentary films. His book, *The Doctor and the Devils*, published earlier this year, is the first instance of a film-script being printed before any film of it has been made. Among his unpublished works are several poems and a radio play, a part of which was printed in the half-yearly Italian review, *Botteghe Oscure*. The scene of this play is a Welsh village, and parts of it have been performed in New York.

Gift for Mimicry

In recent years, Dylan Thomas has made several tours of American universities, giving readings of poetry and lectures. His reading of poetry, and particularly of his own poems (which he confessed that he did not like reading) was unrivalled; and he was almost equally accomplished in reading humorous scripts of an unparalleled adjectival richness, which were among the most popular wireless features of our time. His gift of mimicry could make each character of his stories distinct and unforgettable. He loved people. He did not write only for the few but also 'for the lovers . . . Who pay no praise or wages Nor heed my craft or art.'

Dylan Thomas had intended, before returning to England from this latest tour, to work with Stravinsky on the libretto of an opera. It is likely that by his death the world has lost a masterpiece. What has it not lost in the work of a poet who was able to live Christianity in a public way, and whose work distilled it – a poet narrow and severe with himself and wide and forgiving in his affections. Innocence is always a paradox, and Dylan Thomas presents, in retrospect, the greatest paradox of our time.

He married, in 1936, Miss Caitlin McNamara, who survives him, together with two sons and a daughter.

VERNON WATKINS'S OWN TYPED
ACCOUNT OF HIS FIRST MEETING
WITH DYLAN THOMAS

I. First meeting of Vernon Watkins with Dylan Thomas

(1935; V.W. nearly 29 and D.T. 8 years younger)

We met a few months after his first book, Eighteen Poems,
had been published. I remember turning over the pages of the
book in the bookshop where it was prominently displayed; I was
filled with curiosity - but also determined not to buy it.
But I'd known his uncle when I was a child, and I happened to
meet him again in a Swansea street, and he gave me his address.
Shortly after this we met.

He was slight, shorter than I had expected, shy, rather
flushed and eager in manner, deep-voiced, restless, humorous,
with large, wondering, yet acutely intelligent eyes, gold curls,
snub nose, and the face of a cherub. I quickly realized when
we went for a walk on the cliffs that this cherub took nothing
for granted. In thought and words he was anarchic, challeng-
ing, with the certainty of that instinct which knows its own
freshly discovered truth.

II.

We were both Welsh, both Christian poets; we both loved
the sea and lived by it. We both believed that it was good for
living poets to learn from dead and ancient models rather than
from their contemporaries. We thought that a good poem was one
which could never be fashionable.

He used to send me his poems as they were finished, but
sometimes I would see the poem first at his house and then he
would read it aloud. If a word were challenged, or a line,
he would read it many times, and try over every alternative
on his tongue, softly and then loudly, but repeatedly, like
Verlaine.

His method in composition was painfully slow and became
slower as the years went on, so that eventually a hundred or more
drafts would go into a poem. He used separate work-sheets for
individual lines, sometimes a page or two being devoted to a
single line, while the poem was gradually built up phrase by
phrase. He usually knew beforehand exactly how he wanted it to
be, and he would decide how many lines to allot to each part
of its development. In spite of the care he took in constructing
a poem and making it symmetrical, he recognised at all times
that it was for the sake of divine accidents that a poem
existed at all.

III.

The true tragedy of Dylan Thomas's death is that he died. Everything else is secondary to that. His tours of America may be regarded as a progress towards an inevitable destruction, but this suggests quite a false picture of him as he appeared to me when he returned from them. I used to find him full of health and vigour. The difference between the last tour and the earlier ones is that when he went off on it he was already seriously ill. He knew this, and but for his financial straits it is fairly certain that he would not have gone...

The tragedy of Dylan Thomas's death is made more bitter by the banality of judgment to which it gives rise. Those who were magnetised by his power to entertain became the victims of a mutually enacted delusion. This is particularly true of the American tours. The poet, simple, unaffected, and true, was a person rarely seen by his audience. Their dramatic spotlight at once changed him into what they desired. His stories, his wisecracks they remembered, as who would not? but the surprising consistency of his judgments is one thing they rarely seem to have observed. It might almost be said that he was killed by his own mask, by the grimace which his entertainment produced, by a kind of disgust at the popularity of what he was not.

IV.

    I cannot agree with those who suggest that the public figure
of Dylan Thomas obscures the real person. It was an essential
part of him to be public, and a part of his creed that a poet
should make himself and his work public. I think that the private
figure, 'the proud man apart', was the opposite of the figure
he sought to cultivate.

    He had the faculty of immediacy, of making everything
present, and of becoming a part of people's lives almost before
he knew them; how much more did he do this when he knew them
well. When he went on a journey theatrical stories about him,
each one funnier than the last, began to accumulate; when he
returned, all that theatrical scenery, those props, disappeared,
and it was he, in his intense and essentially calm awareness,
who discarded them.

PORTRAIT OF A FRIEND

He has sent me this
Late and early page
Caught in the emphasis
Of last night's cartonnage,
Crumpled in the post,
Bringing to lamplight
Breath's abatement,
Over-and under-statement,
Mute as a mummy's pamphlet
Long cherished by a ghost.

Who for annunciation has
The white wings of the sheldrake,
Labouring water's praise,
The blind shriek of the mandrake,
Broken shells for story,
Torn earth of love's near head
Raised from time's estuary,
Fed by the raven's bread;
A trespasser in tombs,
He bids the grey dust fall,
Groans in the shaping limbs:
'All stars are in my shawl.'
Who feels the deathbound sighs,
Mocks the Winged Horse's fake,
Toiling, as with closed eyes,
Love's language to remake,
To draw from their dumb wall
The saints to a wordly brothel
That a sinner's tongue may toll
And call the place Bethel.

Trusting a creaking house,
His roof is ruinous,
So mortal. A real wind
Beats on this house of sand
Two tides like ages buffet.

The super-human, crowned
Saints must enter this drowned
Tide-race of the mind
To guess or understand
The face of this cracked prophet,
Which from its patient pall
I slowly take,
Drop the envelope,
Compel his disturbing shape,
And write these words on a wall
Maybe for a third man's sake.

BURIED LIGHT

What are the light and wind to me?
The lamp I love is gone to ground.
There all the thunder of the sea
Becomes by contrast idle sound.

What hammer on the anvil falls?
Who shapes the cyclone to his will?
The moment and the intervals
Gain their estate from what is still.

All hunting opposites I praise.
I praise the falcon and the dove.
Night's intense darkness gives to days
True pictures of regenerate love.

Come, buried light, and honour time
With your dear gift, your constancy,
That the known world be made sublime
Through visions that closed eyelids see.

Come, breath, instruct this angry wind
To listen here where men have prayed,
That the bold landscape of the mind
Fly nobler from its wrist of shade.

Sons of true sacrifice are there.
Rivers and hills are in their hands.
The lightest petal the winds bear
Has mocked the Serpent's swaddling-bands.

And men may find beneath the sun,
Dashed into pieces by old wrong,
A relic, lost to nature, one
Whose passion stops the mouth of song.

THE CURLEW

Sweet-throated cry, by one no longer heard
Who, more than many, loved the wandering bird,
Unchanged through generations and renewed,
Perpetual child of its own solitude,
The same on rocks and over sea I hear
Return now with his unreturning year.
How swiftly now it flies across the sands,
Image of change unchanging, changing lands
From year to year, yet always found near home
Where waves in sunlight break in restless foam.
Old though the cave is, this outlives the cave,
And the grey pool that shuddered when it gave
The landscape life, reveals where time has grown,
Turning green, slowly forming tears to stone.
The quick light of that cry disturbs the gloom.
It passes now, and rising from its tomb,
Carries remorse across the sea where I
Wait on the shore, still listening to that cry
Which bears a ghostly listening to my own;
Such life is hidden in the ringing stone
That rests, unmatched by any natural thing,
And joins, unheard, the wave-crest and the wing.

TO A SHELL

At last, beautiful shell,
Lie there crushed; but the sea
Cannot obliterate yet
Faith I remember well:
A house facing the sea.
Hard and bitterly
Though waves beat on that wall
From the swirling quicksands of debt,
I swear that it cannot fall.

Nor can you drag those words,
Confident in their day,
Down to the unknown deep.
I have a net whose cords
Gather the fallen day
And make the forgotten stay
In all but the detail death
Moves to the realm of sleep,
So strong is the pledge of breath.

And though the magical dice,
Loaded for nothing, toss
All to perdition, left
In darkness, held in a vice,
No white breaker can toss
All to a total loss.
Still the relic will hold,
Caught in a secret cleft,
Tenderer light than gold.

All I remember, all
Of the locked, unfolding days
Where tomorrow's treasure shines.
Fragile nautilus caul,
Tell the fingers of days:
'Find me. Enter the praise
Of Eden's morning, inlaid
With dazzling, intimate lines.
Touch, and the world will fade.'

AT CWMRHYDYCEIRW QUARRY

I

Let the fused boulder crack, the inert weight
In this gigantic theatre pluck new groans
From lithic silence; tongues issue forth from stones
Sullen, rebellious, or reconciled to fate.
How like that circle where Dante's words relate
How spirits noticed the shadow he alone
Cast; here stones rain down, and the rock intones
Tablets from tombs, tomes for none to translate

Yet grooves unwind voices; and he who engraves
This stone, soon in his childhood's park to lie,
Shall cut lines incised like a breathing cry,
And give to stone that undulant line of waves.
But who had guessed, in the hush of many graves
Riven by love, it was Roethke's turn to die?

II

Life seems unquarried before the small stones' hail
And electric storm of rock hurled to the pit,
Silent before the blast, showing after it
Tablets fallen in a mass of stones and shale.
So thunders break man; great undertakings fail
In a flash, and broken lie; then only wit
And a rope held, will harness what here was split:
Through rock facets tenacious secrets prevail.

Between this torrent of boulders and the last
In the valley of giants, knowing no weight can stay
The force of roots, we trample the red clay,
Seeking a stillborn offspring of the blast
From silence freed, by glory of diction paid,
Now needed for his own gigantic glade.

CWMRHYDYCEIRW ELEGIACS

Go, swallow, and tell, now that the summer is dying,
Spirits who loved him in time, where in the earth he is laid.
Dumb secrets are here, hard as the elm-roots in winter;
We who are left here confront words of inscrutable calm.
Life cuts into stone this that on earth is remembered,
How for the needs of the dead loving provision was made.
Strong words remain true, under the hammer of Babel:
Sleeps in the heart of the rock all that a god would restore.

Never shall time be stilled in the quarry of Cwmrhydyceirw,
Not while the boulder recoils under the force of the fuse.
Tablets imprisoned by rock, inert in the sleeping arena,
Quake in the shudder of air, knowing the swallow has passed.
One grief is enough, one tongue, to transfigure the ages:
Let our tears for the dead earn the forgiveness of dust.

ELEGY FOR THE LATEST DEAD

Over this universal grave the sky
Brings to the grieving earth its great reward,
And it was right to lay ambition by,
The strongest will being deep and the way hard.
This body sleeping where the dead leaves lie
Gives back to trees from colours they discard
The patient light of its own penury
Out of whose silence wakes the living word.
And we who wake, who saw the swallows' wings
Seeking the turning point of their own cloud,
Draw to one place his love of vanished things.
It is not this that leaves the heart's way ploughed;
It is the shade the sun no longer flings
Of one who touched the humble and the proud.

When first we met, this is the path he took,
Exchanging thoughts, when, with a sudden look,
He showed Earth shining like an open page,
A myth in his live hand too young for age.
His stubborn zeal transformed archaic skill,
Binding young words old courses to fulfil
Held by the curb of his unvarying soul
Which kept all majesty in pure control
While each excursion gave them fiery blood.
Above this path, high on the cliff we stood
That day, competing who could further cast
A knife-edged stone. That knife-edge whistling past,
Singing through air, hit rocks and water now.
He crouched, and listened for the scream below.

If the wrong world, if man's abuse of man
Cast its own shadow on the race he ran,
Here he forgot it. Here above the slade
Sprang to immediate life his talking shade,
The forward-looking shade accompanied
By all the imagination in its greed
Which, on the long, bare cliff-walks we enjoyed
With living shapes would dramatize the void.

And I recall, one late October day
When, going to bathe, he peopled the whole bay
(It was already dark) with human brutes
Feeding in silence, in correct grey suits,
Compact and patient, one with sanguine sighs
Offering the next a sandwich of dried eyes.

I take the watery glass of hours for theme
Fixed, where the heron stoops above the stream.
His quick imagination in that glass
Could make of every form that he saw pass
A timeless image in the living mind.
Each moment all is judged. No man can find
An exit from the circle he is in
Of time, for timeless vision to begin.
Yet, though all faded, still I count it pure
To have loved the valid fact, made that endure
Which held his heart and fixed the heron's eye.
Who now says nothing says as much as I.
Whatever books men write, when all is said
There are no words to mourn the latest dead.

WHY DO WORDS IN MY EARS

Why do words in my ears
Ring as though they were said
Scarcely a moment past?
Why does the echo last
Sudden, after long years,
Of one so alive, though dead?

Surely there is a place
Which, though abandoned, stays,
Letting the landscape made
By chance or circumstance fade
So that feature and face
May stem the current of days.

THE EXACTING GHOST

I speak of an exacting ghost,
And if the world distrust my theme
I answer: This that moved me most
Was first a vision, then a dream.

By the new year you set great store.
The leaves have turned, and some are shed.
A sacred, moving metaphor
Is living in my mind, though dead.

I would have counted good years more,
But all is changed: your life has set.
I praise that living metaphor
And when I sleep I see it yet.

Why is it, though the conscious mind
Toils, the identity to keep
Forgetful ages leave behind,
No likeness matches that of sleep?

Last night, when sleep gave back the power
To see what nature had withdrawn,
I saw, corrected by that hour,
All likenesses the mind had drawn.

In crowded tavern you I found
Conversing there, yet knew you dead.
This was no ghost. When you turned round,
It was indeed your living head.

Time had returned, and pregnant wit
Lodged in your eyes. What health was this?
Never had context been so fit
To give old words new emphasis.

If hope was then restrained by doubt
Or joy by fear, I cannot tell.
All the disturbances of thought
Hung on my words; yet all seemed well.

11

You smiled. Your reassurance gave
My doubt its death, my hope its due,
I had always known beyond the grave,
I said, all would be well with you.

You fixed contracted, narrowing eyes
To challenge my instinctive sense.
The uncertainty of my surmise
Their penetration made intense.

'What right had you to know, what right
To arrogate so great a gift?'
I woke, and memory with the light
Brought back a weight I could not lift.

In sleep the dead and living year
Had stood one moment reconciled,
But in the next the accuser's spear
Had sacked the city of the child.

Why is it, though the conscious mind
Toils, the identity to keep
Forgetful years will leave behind,
No likeness matches that of sleep?

THE RETURN

I lay, pulse beating fast,
While the night raider passed
And gave each hovering tick
The speed of dream.
Sleep in the dead of night could make all quick,
Reverse the extreme
Outrider's task on thought's magnetic beam.

What life-uprooting year
Sent him, an envoy, here
To set two states at war?
I'ld rather set
Those just names up both states are honoured for,
Lest time forget
He is a hostage since our eyes last met.

Now from that neighbour state
One who all war did hate
Came as a witness back
From that night raid,
To make a truce, there in the very track
Where wings had made
A single engine stop, two hearts afraid.

Yet we could still converse
Without interpreters,
For, though spade's land is charged
With sudden springs
Whose atoms may be monstrously enlarged,
Earth-rooted things
Remain the identities to which man clings.

It is our common speech
Comforts the ghost in each,
So, when that restless face
Returned last night,
It gave serenity to time and place,
Though beams of light
Crossed and converged to pick out wings in flight.

True recognition broke
Destruction's dust and smoke,
For there, unfeigned I found,
Knowing him dead,
Life, not with laurels nor disturbance crowned,
But calm instead.
Compassion curbed the challenge of his head.

Our two states merged in dream's
Converging, crossing beams,
Recalling a lost time
Of death and sighs
When body and soul had shuddered at the crime
Dark guilt descries
In the wronged heaven, against which armies rise.

Strongly they still can merge
Where the long beams converge.
Why let two states at war
Destroy the mind?
These eyes beneath a brutal metaphor
Can substance find
In all time spurns but cannot leave behind.

THE SLOE

Too like those lineaments
For waking eyes to see
Yet those the dream presents
Clearly to me.

How much more vivid now
Than when across your tomb
Sunlight projects a bough
In gradual gloom!

Even such a curious taste
I found, seeing Winter blow
Above a leafless waste
The bitter sloe.

It will not yet begin
To act upon the tongue
Till tooth has pierced the skin
And juice has sprung:

A flavour tart and late
Which, when the rest had gone,
Could hide in mist and wait,
Its root in stone.

THE PRESENT

Strange, is it not, that he for whom
The living moment stood in flesh,
Should bring the future to this room
Held at arm's length, and always fresh.

Strange, that his echoing words can spell
New meanings though the die is cast,
And tell us more than time can tell,
Immediate in a timeless Past;

And stranger still, for us who knew
The living face and now return
Its pictured gaze, so quick, so new,
Love's vital fire being its concern,

To think, though years should gallop now
Or lag behind, he will not care,
So calm the eyes beneath the brow,
Held in a breath by angels there.

THE DEATH MASK

I stop because a footfall with no sound
Passes. The laurel is too young as yet
To feed with berries him it has not crowned;
Nor would he now regret
More tender fingers: praise is not enough,
And though the Sibyl in her rock repeat:
'No, none shall draw his likeness, even in rough',
The death-mask does not cheat.

ENGLYN

Bitter it is to see the noble cast down,
Breath broken, truth taken, while wit, brother to fame,
Hostage stands in each letter
Witness, still, to his calm, till death overcame him.

VULTURES

Fling bones to vultures, who dissect
Thoughts of a living man when dead.
Trust the wide wings to spread his shade
And win what he hates most, respect.

from BIRTH AND MORNING

Are you come then, with the first beech leaves, stubborn and frail,
Dragging new brilliance out of the night of the branch
Where apple-trees move under wind, on fire from the wound of the
    grail,
Stream of wild stars for a fork-stemmed blossom to stanch?

            ★   ★   ★

I restore to the garden the footprints of one that was near
Whose arms would cradle you now, a maganimous ghost,
But who sleeps without knowing your name in the turn and the quick
    of the year.
My eyes are fixed on the branches, my soul on the lost.

            ★   ★   ★

All the morning the lawn has been filled with a woodpecker's cry
Awake in the shrubbery, diving from tree to tree.
The air is green with his sallies. In the wake of his plumage I
Divine with a leaden plummet the days to be.

            ★   ★   ★

Still child, undisturbed by his noise, none asks you to find
The water of life, the stone no philosopher found,
Or the source of that secret river which runs under time and the wind,
Sprung, it may be, from a chalice laid in the ground.

Few are the days gone by since you looked your first
And holy their fingers who laid it, halted in frost
Too early to wake you now to heaven in the apple-tree garden
Near branches knowing nothing of that which is lost.

from THE PULSE AND THE SHADE

His name being said, instantly he appears,
Caught, in a timeless flash, with life's own look
Which none could seize or copy in a book.
I marvel, who had missed that look for years.
Still font of heaven, borne on the moving weirs,
Or christening water in the running brook,
You that restore, by cleansing, what time took:
The man survives; his abstract disappears.

Where is his name's true habitat, so near
In retrospect, and yet so far in state?
An instant's threshold on which angels wait
Still renews time within a timeless year.
Illusions conquered, absent lives are here,
And all is early, though recorded late.

A TRUE PICTURE RESTORED

Memories of Dylan Thomas

Nearer the pulse than other themes
His deathborn claims are pressed.
Fired first by Milton, then the dreams
Of Herbert's holy breast,
Out of his days the sunlight streams
And fills the burning West.

I look where soon the frosty Plough
Shall hang above the sill
And see the colours westward flow
To green Carmarthen's hill.
There sinks the sky of changes now
On waters never still.

Praise God, although a time is gone
That shall not come again,
If ever morning rightly shone,
A glass to make all plain,
The man I mourn can make it live,
Every fallen grain.

I see the house where we would meet;
I see my steps return,
Kicking the sparks of the Swansea street,
And still those windows burn,
Struck by the sunrise hour of life
With all men's lives to learn.

My echoing footsteps when they stop
Reconstitute the town,
That working window at the top,
The neophyte and clown
Setting the reel and arc-light up
To pull illusion down.

The various roofs beneath that house,
The crooked roads and straight,
The excess or strictness God allows
In every devious fate,
He honoured these with early vows
And cursed the aloof with late.

The latest dead, the latest dead,
How should he have died,
He in whom Eden's morning
Had left its ancient pride,
Adam, God, and maiden,
Love, and the yearning side?

And Wales, when shall you have again
One so true as he,
Whose hand was on the mountain's heart,
The rising of the sea,
And every praising bird that cries
Above the estuary?

He never let proud nature fall
Out of its pristine state,
The hunchback fed upon a love
That made the crooked straight,
No single promise broken
On which the heart must wait.

The heron poised above the glass
With straight and stabbing bill,
Among the water's moods that pass
Choosing to strike and kill,
Transfixed the sky with holiest eye
When the whole heart was still.

Down to the solstice moves the sun
And through Saint Lucie's night
Under the earth all rivers run
Back to the birth of light.
Among the living he was one
Who felt the world in flight.

Climbing Cwmdonkin's dock-based hill,
I found his lamp-lit room,
The great light in the forehead
Watching the waters' loom,
Compiling there his doomsday book
Or dictionary of doom.

More times than I can call to mind
I heard him reading there.
His eyes with fervour could make blind
All clocks about a stair
On which the assenting foot divined
The void and clustered air.

That was the centre of the world,
That was the hub of time.
The complex vision faded now,
The simple grew sublime.
There seemed no other valid stair
For wondering feet to climb.

That strictest, lie-disrobing act
Testing the poem read
Which, after toil and plumbing,
Left the first cause unsaid,
Showed me his nature then as now,
The life he gave the dead.

There, near Cwmdonkin, first and last,
Witness of lives below,
He held the unrisen wisdom fast
From heaven in overthrow,
Where lamps of hooded meaning cast
Light on the words below.

And later, in that toppling house
Over the village hearse,
Where the Portreeve assembled
His birds and characters,
It was the dying earth he gave
To heaven in living verse.

In London, when the blinds were drawn
Blackening a barbarous sky,
He plucked, beneath the accusing beams,
The mote out of his eye.
In the one death his eye discerned
The death all deaths must die.

'My immortality,' he said,
'Now matters to my soul
Less than the deaths of others.'
And would not fame enrol
Every forgotten character
If Shakespeare held the scroll?

The latest dead, the latest dead,
What power could pull him down
Who on a breath of vision
Could animate a town,
Could plunder every shy retreat
And give the lost renown?

Not by the wars of human minds
Nor by the jealous word
Nor by the black of London's blinds
Or coffin's rattling cord,
But by the stillness of that voice
The picture is restored.

Let each whose soul is in one place
Still to that place be true.
The man I mourn could honour such
With every breath he drew.
I never heard him wish to take
A life from where it grew.

And yet the man I mourn is gone,
He who could give the rest
So much to live for till the grave,
And do it all in jest.
Hard it must be, beyond this day,
For even the grass to rest.

THE SNOW CURLEW

Snow has fallen all night
Over the cliff. There are no paths.
All is even and white.
The leaden sea ebbs back, the sky is not yet light.
Hidden from dawn's grey patch
Behind frosted windows, ash ticks out faded hearths.

How quickly time passes. There is no mark
Yet upon this manuscript of snow.
Where water dripped, ice glitters, sheaved and stark.
The pen has fallen from the hand of dark.
White are lintel and latch.
Earth has forgotten where her dead go.

Silence. Then a curlew flutes with its cry
The low distance, that throbbing Spring call,
Swifter than thought. It is goodbye
To all things not beginning, and I must try,
Making the driftwood catch,
To coax, where the cry fades, fires which cannot fall.

EXEGESIS

So many voices
Instead of one.
Light, that is the driving force
Of song alone:
Give me this or darkness,
The man or his bone.

None shall replace him,
Only falsify
Light broken into colours,
The altered sky.
Hold back the bridle,
Or the truth will lie.

AFTERWORD

(from *Portrait of a Friend* by Gwen Watkins, Gomer Press, 1983)

> *I hold from heaven the power to see what's gone*
> *So clearly, that what is or is to be*
> *Hinders no whit the noblest I have known,*
> *His passion rooted, singing like a tree. – V.W.*

Not many obituaries of Dylan Thomas made any mention of Vernon Watkins. Every obituary of Vernon that I have seen mentions Dylan, often to compare their poetry. Philip Larkin said in the *Times*:

> He always stressed an affinity as a writer with his friend Dylan Thomas . . .
> Where Thomas was strongly wrought, earthy and even humorous in his
> poems, however, Watkins was abstract, rhapsodic and light in texture . . .

The *South Wales Evening Post* said:

> To few towns has befallen the honour of nurturing two poets of world-
> acknowledged eminence in the same generation. The friendship of Dylan
> Thomas and Vernon Watkins in pre-war Swansea is one of the most famous
> of literary affinities. Neither owed any measure of his fame to the other,
> but both benefited by their exchange of ideas on poetry . . . Yet their
> temperaments and ways of life were very different – Dylan the exhibitionist,
> bohemian and improvident; Vernon the quiet-living bank clerk, respected by
> all who knew him; Dylan burnt out at 40; Vernon, though eight years his
> senior, surviving him by 14 years during which his mystical thought deepened,
> his fame steadily grew, and his devotion to Dylan's memory never waned.

In the book *Vernon Watkins 1906–1967*, edited by Leslie Norris, and containing tributes in prose and verse, twelve of the eighteen contributors mention Dylan, but not one attempts any assessment of the friendship. Hugo Williams remembered

> the unassuming way he assumed himself to be of interest – in long, hilarious
> passenger-seat monologues – solely for his friendship with the ever-present
> 'Dylan'

and this was an impression Vernon also gave his colleagues at the University of Washington – that his sole justification for being there was that he had known Dylan Thomas.

Already in Vernon's lifetime the myth had arisen that Vernon represented a stable element in Dylan's unstable world. Dr B. W. Murphy, in his *Creation and Destruction: Notes on Dylan Thomas* wrote about their relationship:

It is timely to state how important Watkins was to Dylan, who depended on him in several ways. I believe Vernon was the ideal father of Dylan's family romance, and without his influence it seems likely to me Thomas would not have developed personally and poetically as he did, and may [sic] have disintegrated much earlier.

And in the memorial volume Glyn Jones commented on the fact that Vernon was prepared to endure forty years of routine in an unglamorous job to be able to concentrate on poetry:

> This sort of thorough-going renunciation Dylan, although himself incapable of any such single-mindedness, could understand and esteem, perhaps even revere. It is easy to see why he placed so much trust in Vernon and leaned so heavily upon him. In the mounting disorder of Dylan's affairs the serene dedication and the Christian acceptance of Vernon must have seemed like a still centre, a point of unattainable sanity.

Constantine FitzGibbon, in *The Life of Dylan Thomas*, perpetuated the myth:

> His friendship with Vernon Watkins was perhaps, from the point of view of the poet, the most important of his life after Dan Jones's . . . His relationship with Vernon Watkins was henceforth to be close and special . . . he provided the Welsh counterpoint to Dylan's roaring London friendships, but did so with an ease and flavour that Dylan's more provincial Welsh friends, such as Dan Jones, lacked. [In fact, Dr Jones' scholarship and knowledge of European literature were incomparably greater than Vernon's.]

Even Paul Ferris, though admitting that Vernon was 'a strange friend' for Dylan, adds:

> Watkins, eight years older, was a bulwark of some kind . . . a charitable, humorous man who teased out a quieter Thomas.

Only Roland Mathias in the *Writers of Wales* series, referring to 'this odd friendship', warns about

> accepting too absolutely the ranged reasons provided by the mature apologist for his friendship with Dylan Thomas . . .

Yes, and we must beware too of accepting the too easy interpretations of journalists and biographers. Dylan may have needed a father-figure, but he certainly did not want one, and would have run miles to escape from any 'still centre' of 'unattainable sanity'. He wanted people who would supply his needs – money, drinks, amusement and company. He did not need any help with his poems, he had too much confidence for that; it was a bonus that Vernon would discuss technical details, type out the poems, and make him frequent, if small, loans. He kept in moderately close touch with Vernon only from 1936 to 1945, and certainly when I met him towards the end of the war I often had the impression that he was bored with Vernon's company. Of course there were times when he appeared to be affectionate, charming, solicitous; but there were many more times when he was irritable, captious, even rude. I am not saying this was not true for most of the people Dylan knew; I am only saying that I don't think Dylan was capable of a mature or lasting relationship (except perhaps, in certain ways, and for special reasons, with Dr Daniel Jones). And the relationship with Vernon could never be called an intimate one. When they met, Dylan's engagement to Pamela Hansford Johnson had recently lapsed, but he did not mention her, not did Vernon hear of Caitlin until Dylan was actually married. Indeed, Dylan never talked to Vernon about any of his escapades with women, certainly not of the woman called 'Sarah', not of Liz Reitell. Worse than this, he did not tell Vernon that so many of his early poems were taken from the Notebooks, though he had no hesitation in telling Henry Treece, who was never a close friend and whose poetry he despised.★ He cared nothing about Vernon's feelings, leaving letters unanswered, never in the later years commenting on or even referring to his poetry, not turning up to his masque or his wedding. But this is only to say that Dylan was Dylan.

Why did Vernon, a passionate and in some ways unforgiving man, not only put up with this, but always come back for more? I think the answer is simpler than it appears. Biographers have commented on the differences between the two, but this was merely that they were wearing different masks. It was the same man underneath, who had turned from life, which he could not control, to words, which he could. Vernon had merely chosen (or been condemned to, since neither seemed to have any real choice) a 'safer' or more conventional mask than Dylan. Dylan did not particularly care to see himself in a distorting mirror, but Vernon was always fascinated by the more dangerous path he might so easily have trodden. If Vernon's father had allowed him to spend the year in Italy he so desperately pleaded for after leaving Cambridge, he might never have gone into the bank. Might his poems had been better or worse if he had taken some of the risks his friend had taken? Dylan's life might tell him the answer; when that life ended, his chance of knowing the answer was gone for ever.

★ '"In the beginning was the Bird!"!!' he said bitterly to Vernon, of one of Treece's lines. 'There's only one worse line, "In the beginning was the Turd".'

Dylan was his *alter ego*; when he supported, protected, admired Dylan, it was because of the life he had never lived himself. Dr Murphy comments on the extent to which Dylan's friends failed to recognise how sick Dylan clearly was. In Vernon's case, it was not so much a failure as an urgent unconsious need *not* to admit Dylan's many neurotic symptoms, nor the increasing deterioration of his personality and habits. All this was perfectly clear to any unbiased observer. But Vernon stubbornly refused to see these symptoms of disintegration, or, if compelled to do so, refused to admit that they were serious; he called them part of the 'mask' Dylan chose to wear. That Dylan was increasingly helpless in their grip he could not, or would not, see. To do so, to take them seriously, would have been to admit the same tendencies in himself.

Vernon's mask was a different one, but it concealed the same guilt and immaturity, the same inability or unwillingness to cope with practical matters, the same dependence on other people to take care of him. He would not get into debt as Dylan did, because he would have lost his job at the bank; but he frittered money away, had no insurance, and made very little provision for his family after his death. He made a will only because he saw the difficulties Dylan's intestacy created for Caitlin and the children. He did not drink heavily as a matter of course, mainly because he could not spare the time to do so and still write poetry; but he did often get drunk with Dylan. His progress to death seems to me as self-willed as Dylan's; he knew that he had had a serious coronary, but continued to play squash and climb up and down the steep cliffs of Gower, often dragging heavy objects such as fifty yards of fishing net or a sodden tree-trunk. The pathologist who performed the autopsy on him could not believe that he had been playing tennis when he died.

Dylan and Vernon were both forewarned of the possibility of death, and both were helpless to adapt their lives in any way to prevent it; and both of them wrote poems about death to fortify themselves against the approach of death. Who knows how much alike they might have been if Dylan's life had been as closely structured by a regular job as Vernon's was, or if Vernon's life had been as totally unregulated as Dylan's? And who can say whether it was Dylan's death that made Vernon hurry on to death himself?

The quality in Dylan that Vernon most strongly asserted was 'rooted innocence'. It cannot have been harmlessness that he meant, for Dylan, God knows, wounded, grieved and sometimes damaged those he was closest to; it must have been the helplessness with which he watched himself live his terrible life that Vernon saw so clearly. It was that helplessness, which he felt also in himself, that held him so strongly.

For Dylan was like Robin, the marred anti-heroine of his favourite novel *Nightwood*, whose face aged 'only under the blows of perpetual childhood', whose life was 'a continual accident'. The Doctor says of her

> 'And why does Robin feel innocent? Every bed she leaves without caring fills her heart with peace and happiness . . . That's why she can't put herself in another's place . . . She knows she is innocent because she can't do anything in relation to anyone but herself.'

His friendships were in the end transitory relationships of no real depth. But Vernon's feeling for Dylan was certainly the most intense of his life; more than friendship, it was an identification which did not end with death; indeed, Dylan dead exercised an even greater hold over his imagination than in his lifetime. Memories of the past became then so vivid that they seemed at times to blot out the present, and in brooding over them and over the strange dream that showed him Dylan as a continuing presence, he began to wonder whether the tragedy of Dylan's life had been inevitable. He often regretted that he had not remained in closer touch during the last years.

I don't think that in fact anyone could have averted the catastrophe, certainly not Vernon. Dylan did need someone to discipline him; all his life he was like a desperate child trying in vain to find out how far he could go, begging someone to show him what the limits of his behaviour were. But not one of his friends, however much they loved him, was willing to do this. They all indulged him, admired him, many of them even pushed him further than he would have gone by himself, until at last he went too far to come back. Our lives are often conditioned by what people expect of us; nobody ever expected Dylan to live sanely – very few people ever even required normal standards of behaviour from him. Ordinary people had to be on time, pay debts, keep to contracts; Dylan was always indulged, laughed at, forgiven. It is very likely that he would have avoided any friend who did impose such conditions on him. And yet – I can't help remembering how perfectly he always behaved with Vernon's mother, who would certainly never have tolerated discourtesy or drunkenness; how meekly he put back Theodora FitzGibbon's sewing-machine (which he had hoped to pawn or sell) when she ordered him to, how industriously he turned in film scripts for £10 a week. It is a pity, perhaps, that the limits weren't set more often and more clearly.

Dylan's death turned the world round for Vernon. He 'went with half his life about his ways', and the other half of himself was with Dylan. In 1966 he concluded his address to the Poetry Society (in which he talked a good deal about Dylan) with these words:

For the dead live, and I am of their kind.

NOTES

When he was twenty-nine Vernon Watkins met Dylan Thomas, who was twenty-one – an anarchic, iconoclastic cherub; but also, like the young Mozart, a genius, albeit with words, not music. Vernon recognised the genius immediately at that first meeting. All his life he was to reverence it, but he also loved Dylan as a friend. The friendship was not to last long – only eighteen years, but it was to remain in Vernon's memory all his life. Dylan's early death was a grief and a desolation to him. He had always thought that they would grow old together, writing marvellous poems, and 'moving,' he said, 'like Swedenborg's angels towards the dayspring of their youth.'

It was not to be. Vernon never reached old age, but he lived long enough to write the poems in this book for that other poet whom he had loved and mourned for the rest of his own life. There are many many poems in Vernon Watkins' *Collected Poems* which show that the memory of his lost friend was still clear and poignant; but we have included here only those which were written explicitly for or about Dylan Thomas.

The first poem, *Portrait of a Friend*, was composed when Vernon received as a gift from Dylan that well-known photograph in which the poet looks like a young Marlon Brando bent over his cigarette. Because Dylan had simply thrust it into a thin envelope, it arrived crumpled and with a long crack down the middle.

The Curlew is the first of the poems written after Dylan's death. The poet stands on the Gower headland where he so often stood with his dead friend, and the curlew's sweet crystalline cry reinforces the knowledge that never again will his friend hear it. *Buried Light* is also a poem of intense grief and sorrow.

To a Shell was first composed as Vernon walked about Laugharne after Dylan's funeral, looking at places where they had walked or read poems or made up limericks or where they had acted scenes from Vernon's comic *Italian Grammar*, much loved by both of them.

Elegy For the Latest Dead is a long sonnet sequence composed for Oscar Williams's memorial volume *A Garland For Dylan Thomas*. Interestingly, one of the sonnets is a different but still recognisable version of *The Curlew*.

The Exacting Ghost, The Return, The Sloe and *Why Do Words in my*

Ears were all written after a very disturbing dream in the spring of 1954. Vernon dreamed that he pushed his way through a crowded pub to find Dylan leaning on the bar in his usual attitude, with his face turned towards the barman. Exultantly Vernon rushed to his friend's side, and said, 'I always knew that everything would be all right with you, and here you are!' Dylan turned a frowning face towards him, and said with great severity, 'What right – *what right* – had you to think that?' The dream ended suddenly here, but it greatly disturbed Vernon for months afterwards.

The short poems *Englyn* and *Vultures* were written in bitterness against the American press, which after Dylan's death printed gleeful and scabrous articles about him, without mentioning his writing.

The Death Mask is a record of the bronze mask taken by Dave Slivka from Dylan's dead body.

Birth and Morning is too long a poem to print here. It was written after the birth of Vernon's third son in the spring after Dylan's death, and is a celebration of intense joy and sorrow. In the British Library is a large collection of drafts for this poem, containing many very moving lines of grief for Dylan, which do not appear in the final version.

The Pulse and the Shade is another long poem of seven sonnets, each sonnet celebrating a place or a person that Vernon had loved.

A True Picture Restored was acknowledged as a *tour de force*, and was reprinted in many magazines. Vernon was greatly angered by Bill Read's book *Dylan Thomas in America*, which did not show the man he had known.

The Snow Curlew brings full circle the sequence of elegies which began with *The Curlew*.

Gwen Watkins
(March 2003)